TRUST
Unlocking B2B Growth in Today's AI World

How to evolve your GTM model
with authentic connections
to accelerate demand, revenue and
employer reputation

Kristin Oelke

Copyright © 2024 Kristin Oelke
All rights reserved.
No portion of this book may be reproduced in any form
without permission from the publisher,
except as permitted by US copyright law.

Disclosure: Artificial Intelligence was used in the
research for and development of this book.

It is with authentic gratitude and love
I dedicate this book
to Ed, Karen and my entire family,
all brilliant and selfless
in their endless support.

FORWARD

I've known Kristin for several years and have personally benefited from her proven leadership as she ran marketing for one of my companies during an extremely successful period of company growth. At that time, I was deeply impressed as she solved for what others considered to be an unsolvable selling challenge.

To me, obvious elements of her success were her marketing expertise and personal grit, confidence to shine a bright light on the unfiltered actual results (no matter how challenging a given week's results may have been) and her consistent iteration – continually adapting her approach by incorporating what she'd learned to improve outcomes.

Less obvious then, but much clearer to me now, is the focus she had around generating a single outcome – true trust; trust between our customers and our company and with team members who would deliver on it.

That trust was the absolute key for us then and is even more true for us all today, as AI has accelerated the dynamics of potential mistrust, heightening our collective sensitivities to what is real and what is not. I feel that when selling to enterprise clients and pitching multi-billion-dollar investors. I hear it as a Young Presidents' Organization member talking to other CEOs. I live it as a leader myself in working to inspire associates from the C-suite to the front line.

If you want your company to grow in this ever more challenging and skeptical environment, I think you'll enjoy Kristin's vision for building a go-to-market machine that focuses first and foremost on building trust.

-- Davin Cushman, Founder and CEO of Brightrose Ventures and advisor to global investors in the B2B software industry

Contents

Chapter 1
Understanding the Current State of Trust
How We Got Here
Welcome to Today's AI World
The Importance of Trust Relative to Growth

Chapter 2
Reviewing Trust in Your Business
The Connection Between Trust and Being Authentic Evaluating Your State of Trust
The Impact of Decreasing Employee Tenure
The Case for Monitoring 365

Chapter 3
Improve Trust with Customer Advocacy
The Value of Peer Recommendations
Authentic Customer Advocacy
Implementation Considerations
A Hybrid Customer Advocacy Approach: Traditional + Modern

Chapter 4
A Customer Advocacy Model for Today
Use Case: Small Startup Business (with no current program)
Use Case: Established Company (with aged program)
Services Company Versus Product Company Considerations
Incorporating Employer Brand Building
Setting Goals and Evaluating Impact
The Importance of a Company-Wide Approach

Chapter 5
Evolve By Developing a Holistic Trust Model
Core Foundational Elements
Trial, Freemium and Reverse Trial Offers
The Organic Versus Paid Media Debate

Chapter 6
Building Enduring Trust

Chapter 1
Understanding the Current State of Trust

How We Got Here

Have you ever considered that the drag hindering deals moving forward could be that your prospect simply doesn't believe what is being presented to them? Is your sales blocker now more often your prospect's lack of trust, not your product or service capabilities?

I have.

And my research quickly uncovered that leading analyst firm Forrester in their State of Global Business Buyer Trust 2024 Report was also thinking about it. The report revealed that strong trust in an organization is essential and often undermines purchase intent.

The March 2024 PWC Trust Survey also underscores the importance of building trust not just as a moral case, but confirming there is a business case as well, with 93% of business executives agreeing that the ability to build and maintain trust improves the bottom line. 49% strongly agree.

When I combined my pursuit to unpack the impact of trust on deal velocity for my clients, with the two recent reputable research reports that also focused on the importance of trust for business success, as a trained journalist, I knew I was on to something and needed to dig further. What I uncovered was quite a bit of information about the erosion of trust and its business impact, but not many recommendations for what B2B companies can do about it. As a business strategist, I learned long ago, it's not just enough to analyze and understand a trend that is catching speed.

Success is achieved by defining how to harness it, identifying where and how to pivot to take advantage of the disruption.

The fundamental question is what companies should be doing differently now in today's AI world to strengthen public trust with key stakeholders to accelerate both near and long-term business growth? Wherever you are in your journey in thinking about the impact of trust on your business, there's good news that was introduced decades ago and still holds true.

Steven R. Covey, Author of 7 Habits of Highly Effective People, said "Contrary to what most people believe, trust is not some soft, illusive quality that you either have or you don't; rather, trust is a pragmatic, tangible actionable asset that you can create."

Lest you counter that he was talking about trust between two individuals, I would uphold that the trust that a business builds, is due to the actions of its people.

So why is trust eroding and what has changed?

With our increasing reliance on digital platforms, concerns about data security are generally the first things that come to mind regarding trust.

Transparency is also crucial. When companies are not forthcoming about their operations, pricing, or terms of service, it can create suspicion and uncertainty. In fact, in the PWC 2024 Trust Survey, 89% of employees cite they are most concerned with data privacy issues, and it's important for companies to disclose their policies. Surprisingly only 32% of executives say their companies do so.

Trust in B2B relationships is also built on reliability and consistency. When businesses fail to deliver on their promises, whether meeting deadlines, providing quality products or services, or honoring contracts, it can erode trust and credibility. Effective communication is also essential and miscommunication, delayed responses, or unclear messages can result in misunderstandings and erode trust. Ethical lapses or questionable business practices, such as bribery, corruption, or conflicts of interest, can also obviously, damage trust.

Today companies must now ensure high ethical standards for all transactions in both offline and online environments.

Even disruptions in the supply chain, whether due to natural disasters, geopolitical events, or unexpected market shifts, can impact a company's ability to fulfill orders and meet customer expectations. Continual disruptions without effective mitigation strategies can strain trust. In the headlines, we've all seen CEOs attempt to defer blame for negative performance on supply chain problems. Mitigation strategies are important.

Financial instability or concerns about the financial health of a business also lead to distrust. Issues such as late payments, bankruptcy rumors, or unreliable financial reporting can erode trust. Intense competition can sometimes lead to cutthroat tactics and unethical behavior.

Businesses that prioritize short-term gains over long-term relationships may engage in practices that undermine trust, such as price manipulation or intellectual property theft. And, geopolitical instability, trade tensions, and regulatory changes can also introduce added uncertainty into B2B relationships.

Add the fact that B2B revenue models are rapidly evolving beyond traditional sales-led approaches (e.g. increased implementation of product- led-growth (PLG) and ecosystem selling combined with the amount of time that buyers now take conducting research before ever wanting to talk to a salesperson) and the trust equation between B2B companies and their buyers has been in the state of disruption for a while.

Welcome to Today's AI World

Now let's factor in the accelerating adoption of artificial intelligence capabilities to improve efficiency and enhance decision-making. Research from Boston Consulting Group indicates that fully embedded AI is one of the key attributes shared by future-built companies that excel across finance and non-financial measures.

In a quest to fully embed AI and become future-built companies, executives are finding themselves struggling with where and how to adopt. And while AI alone is not the path to success, it is rapidly proliferating across organizations, currently with minimal oversight and guidance.

For sales and marketing teams, companies use AI-powered tools to automate repetitive tasks, such as lead scoring, email marketing, content optimization, and social media management to streamline workflows, increase productivity, and target team efforts more effectively.

For customer relationship management (CRM,) AI tools analyze customer data, predict buying behavior, identify trends, and personalize interactions helping businesses better understand customers, anticipate needs, and deliver tailored solutions and experiences. AI algorithms are also now used to analyze customer data, preferences, and behaviors to provide personalized product recommendations and content, and AI-powered chatbots and virtual assistants are deployed to provide instant support and assistance to customers, answer inquiries, resolve issues, and automate routine tasks.

For supply chain management, AI technology is used to optimize operations by predicting demand, optimizing inventory levels, improving logistics, and reducing costs helping companies enhance supply chain efficiency, responsiveness, and resilience.

For corporate functions, HR and talent management teams leverage AI to automate recruitment, screen candidates, assess skills, and analyze employee performance, streamlining hiring processes, improving employee engagement, and optimizing workforce management.

AI is even applied to financial management and planning tasks, such as budgeting, forecasting, risk assessment, and investment analysis to support making data-driven decisions, optimize financial performance, and manage resources more effectively.

And for risk management and fraud detention, AI technology is utilized to help businesses identify anomalies, monitor transactions, and prevent fraudulent activities more effectively.

According to Andy Thurai, vice president and principal at Constellation Research Inc., in a recent Harvard Business Review article, "{C-level executives} are talking to their corporate governance boards, legal teams and HR teams to figure out the right use case where they can deploy AI and, if so, what things they need to be careful about."

While AI adoption continues at its rapid pace, the concerns about AI also increasingly remind us to ensure our focus remains on the value we deliver to our customers, prospects, employees and other stakeholders, and to not let today's shiny new tool distract us from that.

Enter the role of Chief AI Officer (CAIO,) a role that is being explored as an essential component across all industries to assist organizations with optimizing and guiding the best use of AI.

According to Barry Lowenthal in AdWeek in March 2024, "marketing is where the CAIO position can make the most immediate impact." According to Barry, "very quickly this role will become obsolete. Eventually there will be no distinction between a process and whether AI contributed; there will just be the process. Just like we no longer use www in front of a website address, we won't have to have someone designated as CAIO. But for the time being, we need an insurgent and a champion and very quickly, we won't."

Barry also cites the core CAIO skills to be liaison between departments, lead experimentation and deployment, understand the intricacies of an organization and set standards for success. This sounds an awful lot like great marketing leaders. For your CAIO, or other leaders you tap to tackle your AI strategy and implementation, as far as considering the trust dimension in your plan, transparency is a good place to start.

There are growing concerns about how AI systems work, including their algorithms, data sources, and decision-making processes. When users understand how AI technologies operate and how they affect outcomes, they are more likely to trust them.

Clear accountability mechanisms, such as guidelines, regulations, and oversight bodies, help ensure that AI systems are developed and deployed responsibly. Holding developers and organizations accountable for transparent ethical use of AI technology will foster trust among your users.

Addressing biases and ensuring fairness in AI systems is also crucial for building trust. Efforts to mitigate bias in data collection, algorithm design, and decision-making processes help ensure that AI technologies treat all users fairly and equitably.

Strong security measures and robust data privacy protections are also essential for maintaining trust in AI technology solutions. Users need assurance that their data is safe and that AI systems will not compromise their privacy or security.

Demonstrating accuracy and reliability of AI systems is also under increasing scrutiny. Rigorous testing, validation, and evaluation of AI usage builds trust among users. Consistently delivering accurate results and minimizing errors helps instill confidence. Providing users with control over their interactions with AI systems, such as options to customize preferences, adjust settings, or provide feedback, enhances trust and empowers users to understand and influence AI technology usage that promotes trust and engagement.

Fundamental for earning public trust in AI technology solutions are the ethical considerations, such as respect for human dignity, autonomy, and rights. Ensuring that AI systems adhere to ethical principles and values helps build trust and acceptance within and among teams. AI's impact on trust is multifaceted.

While it is evident that AI can improve team collaboration, decision-making and overall productivity, it also brings about fear and uncertainty among your stakeholders. As a result, building trust in AI technology solutions requires a multifaceted approach.

According to a recent Workday survey, 98% of CEOs said there would be some immediate business benefit from implementing these capabilities, but 43% said they were concerned about the trustworthiness of AI and machine learning (ML.) The study also found that 47% of all business leaders believe AI and ML will significantly amplify human potential, reinforcing there is still much debate about how to today safely derive value within organizations as the AI train is accelerating its speed.

Coupling this with the fact that we're still very early with AI innovation, and especially keeping a close eye on emerging artificial general intelligence (AGI) capabilities and frameworks, what we know so far is that the accelerated adoption of AI in B2B businesses presents both opportunities and challenges for building and maintaining trust. Businesses must proactively monitor the evolution of AI and address the ethical, legal, and social implications that arise. By prioritizing transparency, fairness, and responsible use of AI, businesses can strengthen trust and credibility in our now and forever AI world.

The Importance of Trust Relative to Business Growth

To support business success, taking a proactive approach to building trust throughout your operation, including the incorporation of advanced AI capabilities, may seem like common sense.

But often I encounter executive teams that believe they are effectively addressing this new eroding trust reality by operating in a very similar manner they did 5 or sometimes even 10 years ago, relying almost solely on marketing to drive public trust.

The reasons to do so and the operational changes required to build public trust today are very different from the legacy communications methods and dated strategies still inherent in so many businesses. When you are not effectively maintaining the trust required to be successful today, it can lead to unintended outcomes, which ultimately can impact many key performance metrics.

Customer Loyalty

This is a topic long studied by marketing agencies and academics. According to brand research by Edelman, a global communications firm, 81% of respondents said they need to trust a brand to buy from it. In B2B relationships, a lack of trust can lead to decreased customer loyalty and retention, as customers may seek alternatives they perceive as more trustworthy.

Churn Rate

Businesses with low levels of trust may experience higher churn rates, as customers are more likely to switch suppliers or vendors if they perceive a lack of reliability or credibility. According to the Harvard Business Review, a 5% increase in customer retention can increase profits by 25% to 95%.

Word-of-Mouth

Dis-satisfied customers are more likely to share their negative experiences with others, leading to negative word-of-mouth publicity. A study by Zendesk found that 95% of respondents share bad experiences with others, compared to 87% who share good experiences. This negative publicity can damage the reputation of the business and deter potential customers.

New Business Opportunities

Trust issues can hinder the ability of businesses to secure new opportunities and partnerships. Potential clients or partners may be reluctant to engage with a company they perceive as untrustworthy, leading to lost sales, partnerships, or collaborations.

Employee Morale and Productivity
Trust issues can also affect internal dynamics within a company. Employees may experience decreased morale and motivation if they perceive a lack of trust from management or colleagues. This can result in reduced productivity, lower job satisfaction, and increased turnover rates. According to the PWC 2024 Trust Survey, 42% of executives cite productivity as the biggest risk if employees don't trust their employer and 22% of employees say they have left a company because of trust issues.

Revenue
Going back to where this journey started for me in evaluating the impact of trust on business growth, trust issues can directly impact revenue generation. Businesses may struggle to close deals, upsell or cross-sell additional products or services and maintain pricing power. Research by PwC found that 59% of consumers would stop buying from a company they lost trust in, while 69% would recommend against the company to others.

There are many great examples to learn from and several are shared throughout the book. Basecamp is a good first example to introduce, as it is helpful for seeing very practical ways to improve building public trust aligned to driving growth. This example can also serve as your impetus to begin thinking about and ideating on ways to improve public trust for your business.

Basecamp is a B2B business that offers project management and collaboration software for teams. Start by checking out their website homepage. It's filled with customer quotes, their employee handbook, great analyst ratings, a free trial offer and the ability to directly email their CEO. Another great tactic highlighted on the Basecamp homepage that I will definitely replicate is they conducted a simple one question customer survey asking, "What changed for the better once you switched to Basecamp?" They provide a link to the responses. Thousands responded with an incredible number of very positive comments posted that you, as the site visitor, can scroll through reinforcing in your mind the value of switching to Basecamp. When you have lots of happy customers, this is super powerful and can be easily replicated. Also think about the value for this survey's results across a traditional sales-led revenue motion. Your sellers can select multiple quotes from current customers who are in similar industries with similar challenges and provide the testimonials to existing prospects in your pipeline to improve conversion.

At the time I was researching Basecamp, they also had posted on the front page of their website a message notifying visitors of an upcoming offsite company meeting sharing that their replies may be slower during this time. The full public transparency in advance of the event indicates that they are recognizing the potential customer impact, as well as highlighting company commitment to their team, thus being authentic in building trust with multiple stakeholders.

Chapter 2
Reviewing Trust in Your Business

The Connection Between Trust and Being Authentic

According to the UK-based The Think Tank, the tsunami of AI-generated content has made authenticity a badge of honor and a sought-after quality.

Audiences are becoming smarter and more skeptical as AI-generated content infiltrates the mainstream. Building trust in business relationships is now even more closely linked to being authentic.

Authentic was even Merriam-Webster's Word of the Year for 2023. It can mean "not false or imitation" or "true to one's own personality, spirit or character." When businesses demonstrate authenticity in their engagement with clients, partners, employees, and other stakeholders, it helps build trust.

Authenticity entails aligning words with actions consistently. When your business consistently delivers on your promises and commitments, you reinforce trust. Clients and partners can rely on you to act in a manner consistent with your stated values and principles. Authentic engagement involves being transparent about intentions, processes, and outcomes.

Businesses that are open and honest in your communication foster trust by providing stakeholders with the information they need to make informed decisions and understand the rationale behind business decisions. When you connect with stakeholders on a human level you show vulnerability, share personal stories, or express empathy. This helps build rapport and strengthen relationships. Clients and partners are more likely to trust businesses that they perceive as relatable and genuine.

Authentic engagement involves actively listening to your stakeholders, understanding their needs, and responding empathetically to their concerns. By demonstrating empathy and showing genuine interest in the well-being of others, you build rapport and trust over time.

Demonstrated respect for the opinions, values, and boundaries of stakeholders is another key element for authentically earning trust. By showing your value and appreciation of different perspectives, you foster long-term relationships based on trust and mutual respect. Companies that prioritize authenticity in your interactions are more likely to cultivate loyal clients, partners, and employees who are committed to maintaining ongoing relationships.

As a good example, Salesforce has built its brand around the idea of being a customer-centric company. Their commitment to transparency, trust, and authenticity has helped them become a leading customer relationship management (CRM) platform globally. Salesforce also promotes an "Ohana" culture, inspired by the Hawaiian concept of family. This culture emphasizes inclusivity, equality, and support for one another, both within the company and in the broader community. By prioritizing values-driven leadership and fostering a sense of belonging among employees, Salesforce cultivates transparency and trust within its workforce. By fostering genuine authentic relationships with customers and employees, Salesforce has experienced significant growth and established itself as a trusted partner.

For organizations like Salesforce that operate globally, there are additional cultural considerations relative to being authentic and building trust with stakeholders worldwide. In its 24th year, the 2024 Edelman Trust Barometer Global Report indicates trust is questioned far more if your business is headquartered in certain countries, posing an additional point of skepticism to overcome depending on where your business is based. This, and other similar culture-based studies, can help inform your strategies for building trust and fostering effective cross-cultural collaboration in global business environments.

Evaluating Your State of Trust

For those embarking on understanding how trust is impacting your business performance, a great report I recommend reading is the March 2024 PWC Trust Survey. Now in its fourth year, it offers many good insights. One of the most poignant insights for me was that the trust gap is growing, and business executives continue to overestimate how much they are trusted by employees and consumers. According to the Survey, business leaders are more off the mark today than they were in the last two years.

One reason companies may be overly optimistic about trust levels is that they don't have internal structures in place to consistently identify where the trust expectation gap exists. Many companies say that they measure trust, but those metrics are often subjective and don't fully capture the current sentiment across stakeholder groups such as employees, customers and investors. These often include metrics such as customer satisfaction and employee engagement, which are related to trust, but are only part of the picture when it comes to trust. Companies that move beyond these partial measures can better identify where they should focus.

Common methods to evaluate trust across a variety of dimensions of your business include surveys and feedback, trust indices, employee turnover and retention, observational data, ethical reporting, 360-degree feedback, anonymous reporting systems, performance metrics, exit interviews and benchmarking.

If you don't already have enough of these gauges in place to feel confident about assessing your level of trust with stakeholders, often companies start with basic customer, employee and partner surveys as an effective simple way to identify near-term priorities, establish leadership focus and garner support for new trust building initiatives.

One caution is that it can be easy to over rotate your focus on just the most public issues in a business, as that is where you could have customers, media or employees reaching out for explanation. But the undercurrent of your company's level of trust can be just as powerful for both positively and negatively impacting growth.

The following list can serve well for taking a more holistic assessment across your business, as well as for structure for your leadership or quarterly team meetings.

My recommendation is to prioritize for action the top 3-4 that are most critically important given the current state of your business.

Consistency
- Do your actions align with your stated values and principles consistently across all levels of the organization?
- Are there any discrepancies between what your business claims to stand for and how it operates?

Transparency
- Are you transparent in your communication with employees, customers, partners, and prospects about your business practices, policies, and decision-making processes?

- Do you provide access to relevant information and seek feedback openly?

Honesty and Integrity
- Do you conduct business with honesty, integrity, and ethical principles, even when it's challenging?
- Are there any instances of unethical behavior or deceptive practices that could undermine trust?

Reliability
- Do you consistently deliver on your promises and commitments to stakeholders?
- Can employees, customers, partners, and prospects depend on your business to fulfill its obligations and meet expectations?

Empathy and Respect
- Do you demonstrate empathy and respect in your interactions with employees, customers, partners, and prospects?
- Are you attentive to their needs, concerns, and feedback, and do you take appropriate action to address them?

Customer and Partner-Centricity
- Is your business genuinely focused on meeting the needs and preferences of your customers and partners?
- Do you prioritize customer and partner satisfaction and strive to provide value in your products, services, and experiences?

Employee Engagement
- Do you foster a positive work environment where employees feel valued, respected, and empowered?
- Are employees actively engaged and motivated to contribute their best efforts to the success of the business?

Accountability
- Do you hold yourself accountable for your actions and decisions, and do you take responsibility for any mistakes or shortcomings?
- Are there mechanisms in place to address accountability and ensure transparency in decision-making processes?

Feedback Mechanisms
- Do you actively seek feedback from employees, customers, partners, and prospects, and do you use this feedback to drive continuous improvement?
- Are there channels for stakeholders to voice concerns, suggestions, and opinions, and are these channels accessible and responsive?

Reputation and Brand Perception
- How is your business perceived by external stakeholders, including customers, partners, and industry peers?
- Are there any reputational risks or negative perceptions that could impact trust and authenticity?

Forbes summed it up well when highlighting the first dimension. "Consistency: Anything less than a consistent experience erodes trust. Consistency is where "the rubber meets the road." It is the consistent and predictable above-average experience that gets customers to say, "Wow!" What gets them to that point is when they say, "They are always so helpful ... always so knowledgeable ... they always respond quickly ..." It's the word always followed by a positive comment. Often, those comments are basic expectations. Shouldn't all employees be helpful, knowledgeable and respond quickly? Of course. Just meeting a customer's expectations, with maybe a more positive attitude, will fuel the experience to be better than average. Consistency creates trust. Anything less erodes it."

The Impact of Decreasing Employee Tenure

Several studies from the Bureau of Labor Statistics, Employee Benefits Research Institute (EBRI,) Gallup and the LinkedIn Workforce Report, have documented the decrease in average employee tenure over the past few decades.

Anecdotally, for me, I don't need a third-party report to believe this. From just reviewing my LinkedIn network of thousands of professionals, I can easily see a significant decrease in single employer tenure today from when I first graduated from college.

Today's employees often prioritize factors like career growth, work-life balance, and alignment with company values over long-term loyalty to a single employer. They are more inclined to seek new opportunities if they feel their current employer cannot meet their evolving needs and aspirations.

Advancements in technology and globalization have expanded job opportunities and made it easier for employees to find new roles, and online job platforms and professional networking sites have empowered individuals to explore different career paths and pursue opportunities that offer better compensation, benefits, or job satisfaction.

With the decline of traditional job security and loyalty-based employment models, employees also may feel less obligation to stay with a single employer for an extended period. Companies that prioritize short-term profits over employee well-being, fail to invest in employee development, or exhibit poor leadership may struggle to retain talent in a competitive job market.

As a result, employees are more likely to explore other options that offer greater fulfillment and advancement opportunities. Why is employee tenure important to building trust?

Long-tenured employees contribute to consistency in service, product quality, and customer interactions. This consistency builds trust with customers who rely on your company's products or services, especially for multi-year client contracts with high-touch customer support requirements. Employees who stay with a company for extended periods accumulate valuable expertise and institutional knowledge.

This expertise enhances your company's ability to meet customer needs effectively, leading to greater trust in your company's capabilities. Long-term employees often develop strong relationships with customers, partners, and colleagues. These relationships are built on trust and familiarity, which are essential for fostering loyalty, collaboration and ultimately retention.

High turnover can create uncertainty and instability within an organization. Stakeholders may perceive a company with high turnover as unreliable or lacking in direction. In contrast, low turnover signals stability and predictability, which can instill trust in your company's ability to deliver on its promises over time.

High turnover also negatively impacts employee morale and engagement. Employees who feel valued and supported are more likely to provide excellent service, leading to higher levels of customer satisfaction and trust.

And companies with a reputation for low turnover are more attractive to potential recruits. Job seekers perceive low turnover as a sign of a positive work environment and opportunities for career growth, leading to a stronger talent pipeline and greater trust in your company as an employer.

According to Chief Executive, CEOs who they surveyed in January 2024 were asked to select their top priorities for the year. 60% said retaining and engaging employees is their top priority—a even higher proportion than the 57% who ranked retaining and engaging employees as their top priority two years ago, the last time they did the survey.

Whether the turnover is voluntary or involuntary, decreasing employee tenure creates a ripple effect, impacting trust across various stakeholders. Building trust requires consistency, reliability, and strong relationships, all of which can be undermined by high turnover rates. As another component of your overall trust building initiative, companies should focus on the root causes to offset current and future negative business impact from low employee tenure.

The Case for Monitoring 365

Several of the studies I reference are annual. All are valued, great resources.

But we know a lot can happen relative to growth within 12 months, or even just one quarter.

To best support the now common rigorous growth reviews throughout the year, it is recommended that businesses implement sustained ongoing measurements relative to trust.

There are many benefits for doing so.

Early Detection of Issues

By tracking trust indices regularly, you can identify potential issues or concerns as soon as they arise. Early detection allows you to address problems promptly before they escalate, minimizing negative impacts on stakeholders. A simple example is social and traditional media monitoring. Great tools exist today to assist with early detection.

Real-Time Feedback

Daily monitoring provides real-time feedback on your company's performance and reputation. This feedback can help management including product management, who are often not directly in the feedback loop, make informed decisions and take timely action to maintain or improve trust levels among stakeholders. In-app surveying and monitoring customer support inquiries are great simple tactics that can obtain real-time feedback.

Agility and Adaptability

In today's fast-paced business environment, companies need to be agile and adaptable to changes in market conditions, industry trends, and stakeholder expectations. Monitoring trust daily enables you to quickly respond to shifts in trust levels and adjust your strategies and operations accordingly. This includes having plans in place to know how to expedite actions for replying to reviews on Glassdoor, customer comments on an analyst site, negative earnings announcement or even security breaches.

Continuous Improvement

Regular monitoring fosters a culture of continuous improvement within your organization. By analyzing and publishing trust trends and patterns over time, you can identify areas for improvement and implement targeted initiatives to strengthen trust and enhance stakeholder relationships.

Competitive Advantage

Companies that prioritize trust and consistently monitor their trust levels also gain a competitive advantage in the marketplace. Building and maintaining trust with your customers, employees, partners, and other stakeholders can differentiate your company from your competitors and contribute to long- term success.

To best understand the value of dedicated trust monitoring, let's consider a couple of different hypothetical scenarios.

Scenario #1: Loss of Customer Trust Due to Declining Product Quality

Imagine a B2B manufacturing company that has been in business for decades and has built a reputation for high-quality products. However, in recent years, the company has experienced a decline in product quality due to cost-cutting measures and lax quality control processes. The company does not regularly monitor customer feedback or satisfaction metrics, if their reputation will sustain them. As a result, customer complaints start to increase, and negative reviews proliferate online. By the time the company realizes the extent of the problem, it has already lost the trust of many customers, leading to a decline in sales, damaged reputation, and loss of market share.

Scenario #2: Employee Disengagement Due to Poor Leadership

Consider a B2B consulting firm that has a talented team of consultants and a strong client base. However, the company's leadership fails to prioritize communication and transparency with employees, leading to uncertainty about the company's direction, strategy, and prospects. Employee morale begins to decline, and top performers start to leave for competitors who offer better communication and career development opportunities. The company does not regularly measure employee engagement or satisfaction, so it is caught off guard by the sudden increase in turnover and loss of key talent. This turnover disrupts client relationships, reduces productivity, and undermines the company's ability to deliver high-quality services, ultimately leading to negative impact on business performance.

In both examples, the lack of regular monitoring of trust indices, such as customer satisfaction metrics or employee engagement surveys, result in negative business impacts that could have been mitigated or prevented with proactive monitoring and intervention. Regularly monitoring trust indices allow companies to identify issues early, address them promptly, and maintain trust and credibility with customers, employees, and other stakeholders.

Chapter 3
Improve Trust with Customer Advocacy

The Value of Peer Recommendations

According to the 2024 Edelman Trust Barometer Report "Trust in companies from global powers is in decline and worry over societal threats and establishment leaders misleading us is growing, while peers are trusted as scientists for information on new innovations."

One thing AI can't do yet – influence.

Let's focus on the concept of peers. The term "peer" or "peer group" typically refers to individuals or entities that share similar characteristics, status, or circumstances and are considered comparable to each other in some way. In business or organizational contexts, a peer group may refer to companies or entities within the same industry or sector that are comparable in terms of size, market position, financial performance, or other relevant metrics. Analyzing performance relative to peers can help businesses assess competitive position, benchmark performance, and identify areas for improvement.

Customer advocacy, at its foundation, is about peer recommendations or peer influence.

Now cited in multiple reports, the value of peer recommendations is growing.

In the PWC 2024 Trust Survey, 61% of consumers have recommended a company that they trust to friends or family. With evolving B2B models, coupled with trust-eroding macro market dynamics, buyers are increasingly skeptical about new products and services. As a result, peer authority for driving growth is continuing to increase in importance.

While a lot has changed regarding driving B2B growth over the past couple of decades - selling models, tools, productization and the buyer's journey - there are two things that haven't changed.

1) The goal is to identify where your audience self-educates and get involved.
2) Once you find where they are, plan to stick around for a while.

By implementing an authentic customer advocacy company-wide initiative within the channels where your audience currently self-educates and sharing your customer stories (and other proof points) over time, you can effectively build trust and counter growing skepticism in several different ways.

Inspire Employee Pride and Engagement
- By sharing customer success stories, you can inspire pride and motivation among your employees by highlighting the positive impact their work has on customers' lives or businesses.
- When employees see the tangible outcomes of their efforts through customer stories, it reinforces their sense of purpose and engagement with your

company's mission, fostering a positive workplace culture.
- Think about your own career. What employers inspired you to have great pride in working at their company? Why was that effective and what similar things can you implement within your current workplace?

Build Customer Loyalty and Trust
- Authentic stories serve as powerful testimonials that demonstrate the real-world benefits of your products or services.
- By showcasing satisfied customers who have achieved success with your offerings, you build trust and credibility with existing and potential customers, encouraging loyalty and repeat business.
- When was the last time you (not marketing), without a direct selling intent, shared the good news of your customers and their value of working with your team and your product?

Strengthen Partner Relationships
- Sharing joint customer success stories can reinforce trust and collaboration with partners by showcasing successful collaborative initiatives.
- Partnerships thrive on mutual success, and highlighting joint customer success stories demonstrates the value of working together, fostering stronger relationships and driving mutual growth.
- When was the last time you (not marketing), without a direct selling intent, shared the good news of a partner, and when applicable, the value derived

by your joint customer?

Attract Prospects and Convert Leads
- Customer success stories act as persuasive marketing tools that attract prospects and convert leads into customers, which are most impactful when time to value, resource requirements and quantifiable outcomes are incorporated.
- Prospects are more likely to trust recommendations from satisfied customers and partners than traditional advertising, making success stories an effective way to drive sales and expand your customer base.

Differentiate Your Brand in the Market
- Authentic advocacy initiatives set brands apart in the marketplace by showcasing the unique stories and experiences of being an employee, customer or partner.
- By highlighting the positive outcomes achieved, you differentiate your brand from competitors and position yourselves as a trusted partner that genuinely cares about the success of your customers.

Enhance Recruitment and Talent Acquisition
- Sharing success stories can also attract top talent and enhance recruitment efforts by showcasing your company's impact and culture.
- Potential recruits are drawn to companies with a track record of delivering value and making a difference in the lives of customers, making success stories a compelling recruitment tool.

Foster a Culture of Advocacy

- Implementing a modern customer advocacy initiative encourages satisfied customers to become brand advocates who willingly share their positive experiences with others.

- When employees, customers, partners, and recruits see the value placed on customer success and advocacy, it fosters a culture of advocacy that drives business growth.

As one example, HubSpot, an inbound marketing, sales and customer service software platform, has a dedicated customer advocacy program called the "HubSpot User Groups" (HUGs). HUGs bring together HubSpot users from around the world to network, learn, and share experiences. HubSpot encourages members of the HUG community to become brand advocates by sharing their success stories, participating in events, and referring new customers to HubSpot. This peer-to-peer advocacy helps drive awareness, engagement, and adoption of HubSpot's products and services.

Slack, a popular collaboration platform for teams, provides another good example that successfully leverages peer recommendations and influence to drive growth. Slack encourages existing users to invite their colleagues and friends to join the platform. This incentivizes users to spread the word about Slack to their networks, leading to organic growth through word-of-mouth referrals.

A discussion of the value of peer connections would not be complete without recommending a review of your GTM motion relative to your team's skills for building relationships. Are you only measuring and therefore only valuing conversions? Or have you trained and enabled your team to know how to best build and maintain mutually valued relationships both online and in-person with your key audiences? Make sure you are signaling the importance of strengthening relationships, to then in turn, improve conversions and sustained growth over the long-term.

Authentic Customer Advocacy

Being authentic when sharing customer success for B2B businesses means presenting genuine and transparent accounts of real customer experiences and challenges.

Another way to think about it is that you are working to eliminate doubt among your stakeholders.

Admittedly, this can at times be a bit more challenging for some technical executives and technologists who are not maybe as naturally prone to and comfortable with broad public communications.

However, over the years, I've found there are six key attributes for authentic customer storytelling that serve as good guidance for all team members, regardless of role.

Truthfulness
Authentic customer stories are based on real experiences and outcomes. They accurately reflect your customer's journey, including both positive and negative aspects, without embellishment or distortion.

Transparency
Authenticity requires transparency about the context, circumstances, and motivations behind your customer's experience. This may include acknowledging any limitations or difficulties along the way.

Empathy
Authentic customer stories convey empathy and understanding for your customer's perspective, needs, and objectives. They focus on the human element of the story, highlighting the emotions, motivations, and aspirations driving your customer's decision-making process.

Educational
The most effective, authentic customer stories provide a how-to element sharing insights that can be replicated by peers, including sharing lessons learned and the resource commitment to achieve success. The intent is to share how you helped them succeed and how you can do so similarly with others.

Relevance
Authentic customer stories are relevant and relatable to the target audience. They address common pain

points, challenges, and goals shared by other customers within the same industry, sector, or market segment.

Consistency

Authenticity requires consistency in the portrayal of customer stories across different channels and touchpoints. The narrative should align with your company's brand values, messaging, and identity, ensuring a cohesive and credible representation of your customer's experience.

Permission and Consent

Authenticity also involves respecting the privacy and consent of your customer and other employees involved in the story. You should ensure sensitive or confidential information is handled appropriately and that everyone is comfortable with the content being shared within its context and format.

By being authentic with sharing customer stories, you can build credibility, trust, and rapport with your target audience. Authentic customer stories resonate with prospects and customers on a deeper level, demonstrating the value and impact of your company's products or services in real-world scenarios.

Zendesk, a customer service software provider, employs an authentic customer advocacy approach with a highly personalized website. Upon going to their site, each visitor must provide the size of their organization and industry, which then is the gateway to a relevant customer story being presented that aligns with the website visitor's specific business and serves as the website introduction to Zendesk. These stories highlight how Zendesk's solutions have empowered businesses to deliver exceptional customer service experiences and build stronger customer relationships. Stories include actual quotes, testimonials, and metrics from real Zendesk customers, providing concrete examples of the value and impact of their company's products.

As another example, Buffer, a social media management platform, prioritizes authenticity in its customer stories. Buffer regularly features user case studies, and testimonials with photos, and employee and employer names with their job title, on its website and blog. This highlights how businesses and individuals use Buffer to streamline their social media workflows and drive engagement. These stories focus on the real-world impact of using Buffer, sharing examples of quantitative results achieved and lessons learned. Buffer's authentic storytelling resonates with its audience, fostering a sense of connection and trust with potential customers seeking social media solutions.

Implementation Considerations

In addition to evaluating your current state of being authentic and your current level of trust with your stakeholders, when considering whether it's right for your business to invest in a new or revitalized customer advocacy initiative, there are several factors to consider. These include time, budget and talent, as well as current product and services quality and product adoption.

Time

Availability of Resources: Assess current workload and availability of resources within your organization. Determine if there's bandwidth to dedicate enough time and effort to planning, implementing, and managing effectively. If this is a priority, has it been factored in workload planning? The commitment of dedicated time every day is a critical success factor.

Market Timing: Consider external factors such as market conditions, industry trends, and customer needs. Evaluate where and how your business and success aligns - considering current market dynamics. Are you highly likely to obtain endorsements with the customers and partners in the industries, roles and use cases that will propel growth in your current business climate? If not, why, and how can that be remedied going forward?

Project Timeline: Determine the timeline for launching your initiative and how it aligns with other ongoing projects and strategic priorities within your organization. If building a stronger foundation of trust is important, ensure that there's enough time dedicated to execute it successfully.

Budget

Financial Resources: Evaluate your available budget and current allocated funding. If applicable for your company's customer advocacy plan, consider the costs associated with new or upgraded software platforms, incentives for advocates, marketing materials, and staff training.

Return on Investment (ROI): Assess the potential ROI in terms of increased customer loyalty, brand awareness, and revenue generation. Determine if the expected benefits justify the investment required to launch or relaunch your program.

Cost-Efficiency: Explore cost-effective strategies for building or relaunching. Look for opportunities to leverage existing or new free tools, partnerships, and internal expertise to minimize expenses while maximizing results.

Talent

Skills and Expertise: Evaluate the skills and expertise available throughout your organization. Identify team members within all the market-facing teams with experience in customer relationship management, sales, marketing, communications, and project management who can contribute to the success of your program.

Training and Development: Determine if additional training or development opportunities are needed to equip staff with the knowledge and skills required to effectively execute for content creation writing and technical skills. Invest in ongoing education and professional development to ensure that your team members are well-prepared for their new responsibilities and can get excited and energized about this new important initiative.

Leadership Support: As this requires team members from across the business, ensure buy-in and support from across your leadership team to champion and provide guidance throughout your launch and ongoing implementation. Ensure that there's alignment between the goals of the program and strategic objectives of the organization and that there are shared KPIs and OKRs among leaders, teams and individuals.

Quality

Customer Satisfaction: Advocacy initiatives are reliant upon satisfied customers and partners who genuinely believe in the quality and value of your product and services. Poor product quality can lead to dissatisfied customers and partners who are unlikely to advocate for your brand. This obviously makes implementing an effective customer advocacy initiative almost impossible, thereby eliminating what could be a great tool in your growth arsenal. In addition to case studies, what positive NPS or other customer satisfaction scores, ideally industry leading, have you been tracking that you can publicly promote? If not, what satisfaction scores can be captured going forward with the intent to publicly share in the future.

Product Reliability and Durability: Customers are more likely to advocate for products that perform reliably over time and meet their expectations for durability. Products prone to frequent breakdowns or premature wear may deter customers from advocating for them. Do you have positive, ideally market leading, product performance metrics that can be shared via a customer story? If not, what can be measured going forward for reliability and durability with the intent to publicly share in the future?

Consistency: Consistency in product quality across different batches or versions is crucial for building trust among customers and maintaining a positive reputation. Inconsistent quality may lead to advocacy efforts being undermined by negative experiences. What quality metrics do you track that differentiate you from competitors? Do you have operational feedback loops to resolve inconsistency issues as they arise?

Adoption

Ease of Use: Products that are difficult to use or require extensive training may face challenges in adoption. Advocacy initiatives may struggle if customers find the product too complex or cumbersome. How can ease of use, thereby efficiencies gained by your customers, be amplified via an existing success story?

Value Proposition: Customers are more likely to advocate for products that offer clear value and address their needs effectively. Products with unclear or unconvincing value propositions may struggle to gain traction among potential advocates. Can you bundle several customers into a single story to show - repeated – and therefore more credible, evidence of the value of your product or service?

Compatibility and Integration: Compatibility with existing systems or workflows and the ability to seamlessly integrate with other products can influence adoption rates. Products that lack compatibility or require significant adjustments may face resistance from potential advocates. With SaaS innovation, integrations have been critically important in defining value. Where can you highlight how your product delivers even greater value when combined with another product? If you're not a market leader, do you solve a unique challenge that when integrated with a market leader delivers exponentially greater customer value? By partnering with a market leader and publicly sharing that information, you can get immediate lift in your market.

Perceived Risk: Customers may be hesitant to advocate for products that are perceived as risky or unproven. Mitigating perceived risks through trial periods, freemium products, guarantees, or testimonials from early adopters can help overcome barriers to adoption. In a later chapter, I'll go in more detail regarding the value of trials, freemium and reverse trial products.

A Hybrid Approach to Customer Advocacy: Traditional + Modern

Hybrid models are not just for workplaces in our rapidly evolving world.

Combining the core tenets of traditional customer advocacy with more modern social commerce tactics are establishing a new hybrid customer advocacy model. This new model is increasingly being adopted and showing signs of its effectiveness in building trust to unlock new accelerators for growth, even though skepticism is growing in today's AI world.

Or simply put, you can't keep doing the same thing and expect to get different results. Thank you, Albert Einstein.

For building trust with customer advocacy, what doesn't change is conveying your value through the voice of your customer. What is different today is who communicates what and how often your value needs to be repeatedly communicated.

To better understand the new hybrid model, let's compare traditional versus modern customer advocacy approaches. Pierre Herebul, a LinkedIn Top Content

Marketing Voice who has 94K followers, published a chart that simplifies this. He outlines the difference between marketers and creators. In the chart, he explains that marketers' focus on positioning, messaging, paid ads, website, SEO/SEA and emailing.

Alternatively, creators focus on content creation, trends, social media, influencing, community building, personal branding and building in public. While he claims in 2024 that marketers must learn from creators, I see the value of applying this concept much more broadly throughout an organization.

All B2B professionals, in addition to marketers, I believe have a lot to learn from creators.

By doing so within the context of customer advocacy, your entire organization can better support the acceleration of your company's growth.

For traditional customer advocacy initiatives, marketers generally take the lead working with customer success. Traditional initiatives often involve highly produced content such as formal case studies, professionally edited videos, and webinars. These materials are carefully crafted to present a formal, scripted, polished and controlled narrative. There's a strong emphasis on branding, with a focus on prominently featuring the company's logo and branding elements throughout the content. The messaging is typically tightly controlled by the company, highlighting specific product features or benefits that align with marketing objectives and showcasing carefully selected quotes from satisfied customers that support the company's messaging.

There is and will continue to be great go-to-market (GTM) value derived from traditional advocacy, as core content for websites, social "about" sites and posts, sales enablement, and other company storytelling with investors, partners and recruits.

Often traditional customer advocacy and content is shared through an industry lens, which I have created for several companies over the years with good success. There continues to be proven value when aligning – with the intent of personalization - to your customers by industry, as we also saw this with the Zendesk example.

But the confidence to successfully introduce additional or new solutions within an industry where you already have market traction is changing.

The latest Edelman Trust Barometer report indicates that there is now a clear trust gap between trust in industry leadership versus trust in new innovations introduced. Historically if your prior innovation was successful, accelerated adoption of future innovations within that same industry was considered far more probable given your prior industry leadership.

However, the report cited a clear trust gap countering what has been a long held working principle. This is another signal raising the importance of continually connecting the value of every product to current customer success. (Note: Within the Report, the only cited industry exception where no trust gap existed for adoption of new innovations was within the energy industry.)

Implementing an awards program is another effective traditional advocacy tactic, yet from my perspective it is implemented far less often than it could be. Well-designed award programs publicly amplify advocates as well as strengthen their loyalty and encourage continued advocacy. An awards' program also works particularly well if your happy customers are within companies hesitant to provide company authorization for broad use of their logo or company name in your company's marketing efforts. By recognizing individual customers with awards for their outstanding work, it authentically builds, with real-world examples, awareness for embracing specific issues or solution models, as well as for your products or services. You can easily create multiple award categories that align to your growth strategy, as well as have categories that will generate success stories to help address sales blockers.

One long-running example is the Oracle Markie awards, for which I'm proud to say I was recognized in two different years. Now in its 18th year, this awards program is an excellent mechanism to efficiently capture in-depth customer success stories (that are written for Oracle by the customer via the nomination process.) The program recognizes innovation and use of Oracle's products, as well as supports their valued customers in building their personal and customer company brands. The awards nomination process is also segmented into their product categories and key value propositions, thereby every year easily capturing new stories of current customer use cases that can quickly integrate directly into the existing Oracle GTM motion. The annual amplification possibilities via traditional and social media (promoted via Oracle, the individual winners, and the winners' company social platforms), as well as their websites, are countless.

It is well understood that traditional advocacy has been table stakes for most companies' growth strategy for a long time. What's new is the integration of modern advocacy to establish a more impactful hybrid, company-wide customer advocacy model. This new hybrid model aligns with today's buyer's journey, the buyer's increasing self-education via social media and the emerging revenue models. It also helps to counter growing skepticism about vendor-provided information.

On the other side of the equation, modern tactics are centered on this concept of creators (v. marketers.) This involves such things as user-generated content, including selfies, unfiltered photos, or live-streamed videos, created by customers, employees, partners, and potentially recruits.

Customer advocacy content, traditionally the ownership of just marketing, is now the responsibility of all market-facing employees and partners and is more authentic and relatable. It shares genuine experiences and opinions, often in your customers own words and without the influence of formal marketing editing and reviews.

Social media platforms are currently the primary channels. In fact, according to leading CRM platform HubSpot, 87% of sellers say that social selling has been effective for their business this year. 59% say their company is making more sales through social media this year when compared to last year.

Modern tactics also align better with today's remote and hybrid workplaces, and when adding customer advocacy to your trust building initiatives, customers, partners and employees share their experiences and recommendations directly within their social networks, reaching a wider audience in real-time. Modern approaches focus on creating interactive and engaging experiences, such as social events or live streaming sessions which are all online, where all your stakeholders can interact with each other and with your brand in a more dynamic, personal yet public way.

It's also an effective way to get to know your targets and build trust well before they could be ready to buy. So, when it's time to seek a solution in your space, your company will likely be front of mind as you have an existing relationship established. And when you advance to a selling engagement, there will be greater sales efficiency via an authentic connection with less chance of ghosting, and thereby enabling improved deal velocity.

Word of mouth online recommendation sites are also very important in a modern B2B context. Think of it this way. When was the last time you made a restaurant reservation at a new restaurant without first checking online reviews? The data continues to show that we generally trust the experiences of others over the claims of a company.

Very common in the technology industry is to leverage online analyst review platforms as part of modern customer advocacy and to build social proof. According to G2, one of the top crowdsourcing analyst platforms for technology products, only 10% of B2B buyers indicate vendor-supplied content as "influential" for buying decisions."

Granted there is probably some bias in that statistic as its vendor-provided, but even if we consider only 50% of B2B buyers find vendor-supplied content valuable, you still have 50% of your buyers who are seeking information from sources (highly probable that it's online) other than you.

Another element being reconsidered is humor, which is historically tricky to navigate in B2B environments. In an April 2024 Marketing Week article, Emma Chalwin, the CMO for Workday, a leading cloud-based accounting and HR platform, shared that her company has been on a mission to break from the traditional approach to marketing to cut through an increasingly crowded market. Their shift in focus is away from rational product messaging to humor-filled emotionally driven advertising. To me, this is another signal of the value of human authenticity to better connect with targeted audiences.

Regardless of whether you choose to employ humor or not in your authentic approach, the data backs up the importance of adding modern elements into your customer advocacy model.

The 2024 Edelman Trust Barometer cited online search (59%) and social media (51%) as the two top trusted sources for self-educating, versus vendor-supplied information, which wasn't even in the top five ranked sources.

By combining traditional and modern customer advocacy tactics you will align better with today's multiple revenue models and with your diverse targeted audiences who uniquely self-educate. You can better build trust because a hybrid customer advocacy model leverages the strengths of each method while mitigating their respective weaknesses.

A report from OptinMonster further validates the value of incorporating social media more fully into your revitalized company-wide customer advocacy model. According to its March 2024 data, 87% of buyers think that social media helps them make shopping decisions, 43% of customers learn about new products through social media networks, 66% of customers buy after seeing other people's social media posts, and 71% of people are more likely to buy something based on social media referrals. Overall, OptinMonster cites social selling programs lead to increased pipeline, better win rates and up to 48% larger deals. Whatever statistic is your favorite, if you are not currently maximizing your leverage of social channels to authentically amplify your customer success, it's a missed growth accelerator.

When integrated seamlessly, the two - traditional + modern - can reinforce each other and create a synergistic effect. For example, a successful offline event can generate buzz on social media, while positive online interactions can drive attendance at offline events. Traditional tactics such as face-to-face interactions, direct mail, and events can reach audiences who may not be active on digital platforms. Meanwhile, modern tactics like social media and online reviews can engage digitally savvy audiences (which can include customers, prospects, employees, recruits and investors,) thereby ensuring a broader reach across different segments of your target audience.

This omnichannel approach fosters deeper engagement and reinforces the brand message. The traditional tactics such as in-person events and referrals from trusted contacts lend credibility to a brand. At the same time, modern tactics like social proof through online reviews and influencer endorsements can further enhance credibility. By combining these approaches, you can establish a more robust reputation for reliability and trustworthiness. The power of a hybrid customer advocacy model to accelerate growth is revealing itself in my discussions and new data I uncover almost every day.

However, in the recently published 2024 Digital Marketing Stats from Digital Third Coast, only 36% of marketers are currently attempting to integrate traditional and modern digital marketing efforts. For those of you in the remaining 64% who are not yet attempting this powerful integration, there is significant upside to be had by experimenting with a new hybrid integrated approach.

Chapter 4
A Customer Advocacy Model for Today

In addition to a new or revitalized customer advocacy plan, there are several strategies and tactics that can and should be considered to improve stakeholder trust.

These include hiring a fractional CAIO for optimal AI implementation and oversight which was discussed earlier, and considering new productization offers with trials, freemium and reverse trials to be discussed later, among other trust-building tactics.

But, given my experience, customer advocacy can be the simplest yet most effective strategy to strengthen trust, if the internal energy is created and the resources are committed. The critical factor for success in implementing a new hybrid customer advocacy plan is the company-wide commitment for everyone to do their part - every day.

Use Case: Small Startup Business (with no current program)

For a startup company with limited time, budget, and people resources, who have a few happy customers, integrating both traditional and modern customer advocacy elements into a hybrid initiative is a strategic way to establish broader market trust and accelerate growth. Having direct CEO involvement for closing the initial deal and ensuring ongoing satisfaction through to asking for their advocacy support has been consistently seen to be a critical success factor.

Example: A Startup Hybrid Model

Personalized Customer Testimonials (Traditional)
- To start, your company reaches out to existing customers, who are early adopters, and requests personalized testimonials. A great example for inspiration is the customer story page of Bizzabo, an event management software company.
- Your customer testimonials and stories should highlight the specific customer challenges, how you helped solve them, and the positive outcomes they've experienced by working with your company. For startups, as you often don't yet have many customers, focus on capturing more depth of success with your existing customers, that you can share in long and shortform, multi-purposing each story in a variety of asset formats across your GTM motion as you continue to build your business.
- A simple cost and time-efficient process is to record your customer conversation using your current video conferencing tools and then using the transcript to edit into long and short form testimonials. Ask questions about quantitative and qualitative outcomes, regarding your product, service and company. With all your interviewed customers, ask the same questions, so that you can combine multiple customers on a single topic which is more powerful than a single customer voice. Tip: Record it with only the customer on video. You should remain audio-only which makes it far easier for amateur video editing. Testimonial tools to explore for non-video editing experts for website and media campaigns currently include Canva, Figma,

and Adobe Express (Adobe Spark), among many others.

CEO LinkedIn Initiative (Hybrid)
- By their title, CEOs innately have at least some higher-level of public authority already established. This is a key point of leverage for startups. Often, they are also founders, which through their innovative thinking and courage to start the business, also garner better online LinkedIn engagement than other CEOs who may not yet have those elements of public authority.
- Your CEO can interview customers to implement the first bullet noted above and then post to their personal LinkedIn. Over time, trust in your CEO will heighten by sharing among her thought leadership posts, these customer stories and other proof points, as well as their thought leadership perspectives on industry trends and news. This also supports community building as those interviewed, and those self-educating or wanting to be interviewed, will continually view your CEO posts over time. You'll also start to see a growing following upon which to formulate more ways to interact meaningfully with your emerging community, including identifying additional ways to provide them value.
- For CEO customer meetings, post and share public thank you messages, insights gleaned and the interesting things your customers are doing with your product. Of course, it doesn't need to be for every meeting, but every couple of days would provide that drumbeat of reinforcing information to authentically

instill why customers should stay and new prospects should join. You can also bundle several conversations into a single post with one theme of insights. You are also helping your customers build awareness and demand for their product.
- Most important for the success of a CEO LinkedIn initiative is the commitment from your CEO for (almost) daily authentic contribution and engagement on the platform and ensuring the ongoing addition of all customers and prospects to their LinkedIn network. Every week I see data from early-stage CEOs, and an increasing number of their leaders, sharing the impressive outcomes generated via their personal LinkedIn initiative, most often citing improvements realized for demand generation, deal acceleration and recruiting.

Interactive Virtual Events (Hybrid)
- Your company hosts interactive virtual events, such as webinars or Q&A sessions, where customers, partners and prospects can connect with your team, and ask questions positioning you and your company as a thought leader.
- From my experience, establishing a predictable sustained series, improving the content and process through repeated iteration, will build an audience. If you are not intending to create a repeatable series integrating both traditional and modern elements, I would not recommend this. I've seen minimal ROI from a single-threaded event, either offline or online. If you are willing to commit the time, it can consistently

deliver solid results for both generating new and advancing existing pipelines.

Website (Hybrid)
- For your website, a simple yet effective tactic is to share the backstory on why your business was started. Especially if its family owned. Data shows there is high trust for family-owned businesses. Focus on your mission. Share who is your founder, authentically and transparently.
- This allows customers, partners, employees and recruits to become more emotionally attached to your vision. Include the website link on all leadership and hiring manager LinkedIn profiles, as well as all social media company pages. Despite limited resources (budget, time and talent,) your company's new authentic customer advocacy approach fosters trust and credibility. As a result, you will also drive increasing engagement levels, enhance brand visibility, and improve recruitment efforts that are aligned with the current available resources, while establishing a foundation that is easily scalable as your business evolves.

Use Case: Established Company (with aged program)

Most companies have done some customer advocacy work, but many haven't yet embarked on incorporating the modern tactics now increasingly being leveraged to improve trust and accelerate growth. For the larger and especially cross-functional teams, it is recommended to have your most senior leader host a more formal launch training to ensure all team members know the importance of the new initiative, are educated on recommended processes and messaging, and have an opportunity to ask questions.

Example: Scaling to a Hybrid Customer Advocacy Model

Refreshed Case Studies and Testimonials (Traditional)
- Company revisits existing customer stories and updates with new customers, as well as fresh data, testimonials, and quotes, ensuring alignment with the company's existing product and service offerings, currently targeted industries and use cases, and existing market dynamics and trends. A great example for inspiration is the customer case study page for Hootsuite, a social media management platform.
- By refreshing both format and content, you will ensure you showcase continued relevance and success in solving the ever-emerging current challenges within your market.

UGC Content and Social Media Campaigns and Engagement (Modern)
- Company leaders encourage its customer base to share their experiences on social media via user-generated content (UGC.) You can host a small event yourself or adjacent to an industry event - offline or online - to capture live customer sentiment leveraging the many now free (or very low cost) content creation video and social media tools.

- Employees, customers and partners are invited to post screenshots of their favorite features, share success stories, or even record short video testimonials. Employees are encouraged to augment with key company and product messages and assets within their employee posts.
- Engagement can be on social media or analyst sites. Note that for analyst sites, there is generally a minimum number of reviews required before your company profile is available for public viewing. It's best to pursue analyst reviews once you have at least ten happy customers who would be willing to share their sentiment on one analyst platform. It's also recommended to prioritize one analyst site when extending your request to your customers, so you can accumulate enough reviews in one place to then enable your site to be publicly available. Once publicly available, you can incorporate into sales presentations, via social platforms and on your website.
- A critical success factor is that all market-facing employees continually hydrate their social networks ensuring they are connected to and then in regular contact via the platform(s) with key prospect, customer and recruit contacts so that social media algorithms will prioritize sharing their posts with key target audience members.

Awards Program (Hybrid)
- Design an award framework that would recognize those individuals or teams who are innovating with great success with your product, in areas where you want to accelerate growth.

- Conduct research to determine if any similar award programs exist that would conflict with your customer set or from which you can leverage to inform the structure of your awards program. The intent is to ensure your program is differentiated from any others in the market that could also be recognizing your customers.
- Based on your internal and external research, scope the program to recognize one or more customer success stories to then amplify via traditional and social media channels. Incorporate into your company's key events to add new energy and anticipation for your awards program, as well as to provide additional in-person recognition for your awardees.
- Amplify prior year award winners in your current year call for nomination communications. Conduct extensive promotions during the week of announcing winners, followed by long-form stories of each of the winners for weeks or even months after the actual award announcement.

Partner Collaboration and Joint Marketing Initiatives (Hybrid)
- Company collaborates with established strategic partners and industry associations to co-create content and joint marketing initiatives. This includes events for creation of selfies and live streaming collectively with customers, partners and your company that can be shared via social channels. Look for opportunities to up-level your participation in, or support of, partner events. Identify opportunities to invite partners and industry partners to engage in your events via more

modern, as well as traditional advocacy engagement. This applies to small group meetings, customer meetings, executive meetings, sales blitz days, et al. By experimenting and integrating with traditional and modern customer advocacy elements, a more mature organization can revitalize its customer advocacy initiative leveraging both existing and more innovative approaches to build stronger, authentic and transparent trust across stakeholder groups.

Services Company Versus Product Company Considerations

Customer advocacy models can vary between a product company and a services company due to the nature of your offerings and customer interactions.

Product companies typically focus on highlighting the features, functionalities, and use cases of your products. Strategies may involve showcasing how customers use your product to solve specific problems or achieve outcomes through traditional case studies and testimonials. Product companies often leverage visual content such as product demos, videos, and screenshots to demonstrate the value and capabilities of your offerings.

Implementation for product companies may involve creating visually appealing content that showcases the product in action and communicates its benefits effectively to customers and prospects, now with an increasing number of product companies exploring the use of trials, freemium and reverse trial products. Product companies may also create user communities, forums, or online groups where customers can interact with each other, share tips, and exchange best practices. Implementation may involve facilitating community engagement through online platforms, hosting user meetups, and encouraging user-generated content.

Product companies also may implement incentivized referral programs to encourage existing customers to refer new users to your product, and may involve offering discounts, rewards, or exclusive benefits to customers who refer new business, leveraging modern referral marketing platforms to track and manage referrals.

In contrast, services company customer advocacy initiatives typically involve highlighting how services were customized to meet client needs including overcoming challenges and deliver tangible results. Services companies often position themselves as experts and thought leaders in their respective fields, sharing insights, best practices, and industry trends. Implementation may involve creating thought leadership content such as whitepapers, blog posts, and webinars that demonstrate expertise and provide value to clients and prospects, prioritizing consultative engagement and relationship building with clients. They focus on understanding their unique needs and delivering personalized solutions. Implementation may involve hosting client workshops, strategy sessions, and networking events to foster collaboration, trust, and long-term partnerships.

Modern customer advocacy elements would include publicly promoting these activities to the broader market.

There are also several key factors differentiating how trust is evaluated between a product or service company.

Product companies offer tangible goods that customers can see, touch, and experience directly. In contrast, service companies provide intangible offerings such as expertise, skills, and experiences.

Trust in product companies may be influenced by factors such as product quality, durability, and performance, while trust in service companies may be based on factors such as competence, reliability, and responsiveness. For example, customers may expect products to perform as advertised and meet their needs reliably over time. In contrast, customers may expect services to be delivered promptly, accurately, and with a high level of professionalism.

Product companies may have fewer direct interactions with customers after the initial purchase, while service companies may have ongoing relationships with customers through repeated interactions and engagements. Trust in service companies may also be influenced by the quality of these ongoing interactions and the perceived value delivered over time.

Purchasing a physical product carries risks related to product defects, malfunctions, or returns, while purchasing a service includes risks related to service quality, reliability, or satisfaction. And trust in product companies may be influenced by factors such as warranties, return policies, and customer support, while trust in service companies may be influenced by factors such as service guarantees, testimonials, and referrals.

Overall, while the fundamental principles of trust-building apply to both product and service companies, there are differences in how trust is perceived and established depending on the nature of your offering, customer expectations, relationship dynamics, and risk perception. Regardless of whether you offer products or services, prioritizing transparency, reliability, consistency, and customer-centricity can help build and maintain trust with customers over time.

Incorporating Employer Brand Building

Michael C. Bush, CEO of Great Place to Work, a global authority on workplace culture, stresses the pivotal role that AI has in binding employees and organizations together. More than an abstract concept, he says, trust is necessary for an environment where everyone feels valued and heard. The same goes for AI implementation.

Bush further explains, "If I could create a backdrop for the world right now, I'd spell out the word trust as large as I could. That's what the conversation around AI and workplace dynamics is all about. Employees must understand how AI affects their workflows to fully embrace its potential, and this culture of trust must extend to building confidence in AI systems."

It cannot be overstated that employees operating in an environment that lacks trust are less engaged and productive. Employee engagement has fallen to its lowest point in 11 years, according to a new Gallup analysis, with Gen Z employees showing the biggest drop. Gallup findings indicate disengaged employees have a 37% higher absenteeism rate, resulting in 18% lower productivity and 15% lower profitability. A focus on employer branding, and the foundational programs of both employee and talent acquisition experience, can help address this decline, among providing additional benefits.

For attracting top talent, a strong employer brand enhances your company's reputation as an employer of choice, making your business more attractive to top talent. When candidates perceive a company positively as an employer, they are more likely to trust your company's leadership and culture, leading to increased interest in joining your organization. To support employee engagement and retention, a positive employer brand fosters a sense of pride and belonging among employees, leading to higher levels of engagement and retention. When employees trust their employer and feel valued and supported, they are more likely to stay with the company long-term, reducing turnover and associated costs.

Focusing on your employer brand also ensures that your company's internal culture and values align with your external brand image. And, when your employees believe in your company's mission and values, they are more likely to embody those values in their interactions with customers, partners, and other stakeholders, leading to greater consistency and authenticity in the brand experience.

Employees who are engaged and committed to their company are more likely to deliver exceptional customer service and contribute positively to your customer experience. Customers are more likely to trust and remain loyal to your company when they interact with knowledgeable, passionate employees who embody your brand's values.

A strong employer brand can also enhance a company's credibility and attractiveness as a partner. Companies with a positive reputation as employers are more likely to be seen as trustworthy and reliable partners, leading to increased collaboration and partnership opportunities. And a positive employer brand can extend beyond the workplace to the broader community. Companies that are perceived as good employers and corporate citizens are more likely to earn the trust and support of local communities, leading to positive relationships with stakeholders outside the organization.

Under your employer brand development umbrella, employers should also review management capabilities and leadership performance. This is highlighted by another interesting insight from the 2024 PWC Trust Survey that cited 86% of executives say they highly trust their employees, but only 60% of employees feel trusted. To assist in accurately understanding your level of employee trust and where you can improve, it is helpful to understand the various root causes that cause the perceptions of distrust among employees.

If leaders don't communicate openly about decisions, processes, or information, employees may perceive this as a lack of trust. When employees feel kept in the dark, they may assume the worst and believe that their leaders don't trust them with important information. Even if leaders verbally express trust, micromanaging behaviors can convey the opposite message. Constant monitoring, excessive control, and second- guessing can undermine employees' confidence and make employees feel distrusted. Mixed signals from leaders can confuse employees. For instance, if a leader delegates tasks but then constantly checks in or overrides decisions, it can create a sense of distrust. Consistency in behavior is also crucial for building trust.

Previous instances of distrust or betrayal, whether within the current organization or in past workplaces, can lead employees to be more sensitive to signs of distrust. These experiences can make it challenging for employees to trust even when trust is genuinely extended.

If employees perceive that trust, and opportunities are not distributed equally among team members, it can breed feelings of distrust. This can occur if certain individuals are consistently given more responsibility or autonomy, leading others to believe they are not trusted as much.

Misinterpretation of communication or lack of clarity in expectations is another area to focus on as it can lead employees to assume they are not trusted. Unclear directives or ambiguous feedback can fuel doubts about their abilities, or the level of trust placed in them.

Organizational culture overall also plays a significant role in shaping perceptions of trust. In cultures where hierarchy is deeply ingrained or where there's a history of top-down decision-making, employees may naturally be more skeptical of expressions of trust from leaders. If employees don't feel recognized or appreciated for their contributions, they may interpret this as a lack of trust in their capabilities. Feeling undervalued can erode trust in leadership and in the organization as a whole.

Employer branding is evolving alongside workplace evolution. Addressing today's root causes of trust (or lack thereof) requires a combination of clear communication, consistent behavior, empowerment, and creating an inclusive and transparent work environment where trust is fostered through actions as well as words.

Setting goals and evaluating impact

Companies should begin the process of setting goals and evaluating impact by first identifying the overarching business objectives relative to building trust that the initiatives should support. These objectives could include increasing revenue, reducing customer churn, expanding market share, or enhancing brand reputation.

To help in setting your goals, and build more energy around making a change to a new hybrid model, a great example of effort to output was shared in a recent LinkedIn post by Sam Jacobs, CEO of Pavilion, a community-powered learning solution. He posted that over the last 18 months he's spent 200+ hours growing his LinkedIn following, and he shared the 6 biggest benefits for doing so: Deeper connections to customers, higher win rates, brand awareness, tighter more aligned partnerships, improved brand voice and helping people. I particularly love the last one. Sam is also the Co-Host of Topline Podcast and a WSJ

Bestselling Author of "Kind Folks Finish First." For all six benefits he shared, I've found these are also the common goals of many of the leaders I work with and provides further evidence that improving how each of us engages in more public social ways contributes to building trust and achieving improved business outcomes.

To start, as a reminder, set specific, measurable, achievable, relevant, and time-bound (SMART) goals.

For example:

- Increase revenue generated from advocacy-driven leads by 20% within the next six months.

- Reduce customer churn rate by 15% through enhanced advocacy-driven customer retention efforts by the end of the year.

- Grow brand visibility by increasing social media engagement and mentions by 25% in the next quarter.

- Generate a 30% increase in qualified leads through customer referrals within the next three months.

Measuring the success of hybrid customer advocacy initiatives involves tracking various metrics and business outcomes related to the use of customer logos, testimonials, videos, social posts, and other advocacy efforts.

As a practical guide, here are several common ways to measure your effectiveness.

Impact on Sales and Revenue
- Track the number of leads generated or deals influenced by customer advocacy content, such as testimonials or case studies.
- Measure the conversion rates and deal sizes of leads influenced by customer advocacy compared to other leads.
- Calculate the revenue generated from deals attributed to customer advocacy efforts.

Customer Retention and Loyalty
- Monitor customer retention rates among those who have engaged with customer advocacy content.
- Survey customers to assess their satisfaction levels and likelihood to renew or recommend the product/service based on advocacy efforts.

Brand Awareness and Perception
- Analyze metrics such as website traffic, social media engagement, and brand mentions to gauge the reach and impact of customer advocacy content.
- Conduct brand perception surveys to measure changes in brand sentiment and perception resulting from customer advocacy efforts.

Content Performance
- Monitor website analytics to see how customer advocacy content contributes to overall engagement and conversion rates.

- Track engagement metrics (e.g., views, likes, shares) for customer testimonial videos, case studies, and social media posts.

Customer Feedback and Insights
- Gather feedback from customers who have participated in advocacy activities to understand their experience and satisfaction levels.
- Use qualitative data from customer interviews or surveys to identify insights and improvement opportunities for advocacy content.

Partnership and Collaboration Impact
- Assess the impact of customer advocacy on partner relationships and collaborations, such as joint marketing efforts or referrals.
- Track metrics related to partner sentiment, satisfaction, and engagement resulting from advocacy initiatives.

Employee Engagement and Advocacy
- Measure employee engagement with customer advocacy initiatives, such as participation in sharing customer stories or providing testimonials.
- Monitor internal feedback and sentiment to gauge the effectiveness of employee advocacy programs in promoting customer success stories.

Community and Social Impact
- Evaluate the social impact of customer advocacy initiatives, such as contributions to community causes or charitable efforts.

- Track metrics related to social responsibility and corporate citizenship resulting from advocacy activities.

By analyzing these metrics and business outcomes relative to your stated advocacy goals, you can then also effectively measure the success of advocacy for improving ARR, NRR, customer churn, CAC, CLV, partner sentiment, top talent recruitment or other core key performance indicators for your business.

If you are just getting started or looking to revitalize your initiative, there are several free and low-cost online tools that can be helpful.

Google Analytics
Google Analytics is a powerful tool for tracking website traffic, engagement metrics, and conversions. It can provide insights into how customer advocacy content, such as testimonials or case studies, is driving traffic to your website and influencing user behavior.

Social Media Analytics Tools
Platforms like Facebook Insights, X Analytics, and LinkedIn Analytics offer free analytics tools to track engagement metrics, audience demographics, and content performance on social media. These tools can help measure the impact of customer advocacy efforts on social media platforms.

SurveyMonkey
SurveyMonkey is a popular survey tool that allows you to create and distribute surveys to gather feedback

from customers and stakeholders. You can use SurveyMonkey to measure customer satisfaction, brand perception, and the effectiveness of customer advocacy initiatives through custom surveys. They also offer 150+ expert written free survey templates that you can customize.

Google Alerts
Google Alerts is a free tool that allows you to monitor mentions of your brand, products, or key topics online. By setting up alerts for relevant keywords related to your customer advocacy initiatives, you can track online conversations, media coverage, and sentiment around your brand. It's simple to set up and can provide you daily articles, blogs or scientific research that match your search criteria to also inform creating your thought-leadership content or to include with your social posts bringing more depth to your posts, as well enabling more frequent quality posts by saving you research time. Tip: Executives often set up alerts on their name to receive notifications when they are publicly mentioned.

Bitly
Bitly is a URL shortening service that also offers link tracking and analytics features. By using Bitly for your customer advocacy content, you can track click-through rates, referral sources, and other engagement metrics to measure the effectiveness of your advocacy efforts. And for creating your content, is there anything more unsightly than long website links?

Google Data Studio
Google Data Studio is a free data visualization tool that allows you to create interactive dashboards and reports using data from multiple sources, including Google Analytics, social media platforms, and third-party tools. You can use Data Studio to consolidate and analyze data from various sources to measure the overall impact of your customer advocacy initiatives.

HubSpot CRM
HubSpot offers a free CRM (Customer Relationship Management) tool that includes basic reporting, and analytics features to track interactions with customers and prospects. While more advanced features may require a paid subscription, the free CRM can still be useful for tracking customer engagement and measuring the success of advocacy efforts.

These are just a few examples of the many free online tools that are now available to help measure the success of your customer advocacy initiative and overall trust-building efforts. By following several of the thought leaders mentioned in this book, it's also a great way to learn early about emerging free or low cost tools with new capabilities.

Depending on your specific goals and objectives, you most likely will need to use a combination of these and other tools to track and analyze your impact across different channels and touch points.

The Importance of a Company-wide Approach

Trust building today requires a team effort, and mobilizing your company should be considered one of the most important success factors for achieving your intended objectives. You will need to generate the energy and commitment for a company-wide approach, especially with all market-facing team members.

Your new initiative will encompass many more employees than the historic blended customer advocacy teams of marketing and customer success (CS.) But keep in mind that marketing and CS team members can serve as great champions to initially showcase the new intended behavior that your now broader, much larger, company-wide customer advocacy team can replicate.

In addition to establishing a company focus, it's also important to define more broadly the ownership of its success for building trust. The PWC 2024Trust Survey cited a lack of clear ownership of trust among leaders, with 24% of executives indicating it as a top-three challenge, up 10 points from 2023. According to the report, the lack of ownership reflects an opportunity for companies to clarify that trust should not be relegated to a single leader.

Instead, it should be everyone's responsibility, with clear objectives, metrics and incentives. In that way, trust is a team effort with key roles for the CEO, CHRO, COO, CMO, CFO and business unit heads. With ownership defined, business objectives must also be aligned among the functions and all team members must understand how strong trust can accelerate growth and a decrease in trust can negatively impact the business.

As a reminder, we recommend a company-wide kick-off event, online or in-person, to educate on the importance of everyone's commitment to action and to build the internal energy for a most successful launch. As part of the launch, it's important to clearly explain how each department plays an important role in contributing to the overall success ensuring understanding of the broader business objectives such as revenue growth, customer retention, and brand reputation.

It's also essential for all departments to be aligned on messaging and brand values to ensure consistency across all touchpoints, from sales interactions to product usage to customer support. Your company must understand it involves engaging with customers, partners and prospects authentically and transparently at every stage of the customer journey, from awareness to sales interactions to ongoing support and beyond, and then appropriately and publicly sharing points of success to evangelize your company's value.

Also necessary is creating an ongoing feedback loop across your company to provide invaluable insights for identifying areas for improvement and innovation, specifically product innovation. By also involving product development teams in the advocacy process, companies iterate more quickly and enhance their offerings based on real customer needs and preferences, thus enhancing product innovation efficacy.

One common point of pushback that I've heard is questioning why marketing simply can't continue to lead your company's customer advocacy initiative.

First, a B2B sale generally is not won by influencing a single person, and especially not an enterprise B2B sale, and neither should be your plan to influence the capture of that deal.

There is added value when you have more of your team engage with more of your prospect's buying team.

Further, a marketing-driven approach often only focuses solely on promoting the company's products or services, rather than addressing broader customer needs and concerns which can be done better with your broader team in support. A narrow marketing focus can also result in missed opportunities to build deeper relationships with customers (via all your employees who are closely connected with customers and partners) and address issues that go beyond marketing messaging.

Customers also increasingly perceive vendor-provided marketing-driven information as inauthentic or insincere if they feel that they are only being targeted for promotional purposes. This can undermine trust and credibility with some customers, leading to decreased effectiveness of marketing campaigns. When customer advocacy efforts are driven solely by the marketing department, other departments within your company also tend to not be aligned in their approach to serving customers. This can then result in a fragmented customer experience, with inconsistencies in messaging, service delivery, and overall brand perception.

A marketing-driven approach often prioritizes outward-facing communication and promotion, while overlooking internal processes and systems that impact the customer and employee experience. This can result in missed opportunities to identify and address underlying issues that are affecting satisfaction, loyalty and trust.

Marketing-driven customer advocacy efforts also may be more reactive in nature, responding to feedback or complaints as they arise, rather than having those in your leadership team who are closest to customers and employees proactively anticipating and addressing needs.

This can lead to a less proactive and strategic approach to advocacy, with missed opportunities to differentiate your brand. And marketing-driven customer advocacy efforts may be more focused on short-term goals due to how KPIs and OKRs are assigned to marketing teams, such as increasing sales or generating leads, rather than long-term relationship building and brand loyalty. This can result in a lack of sustained investment in building meaningful and enduring connections with whom you need to build strong trust to accelerate growth.
In contrast, by implementing a modern hybrid company-wide customer advocacy approach you are engaging employees across all your departments focused on prioritizing and championing customers. This approach can lead to a more holistic and integrated customer advocacy initiative, that will both build a happy growing customer base and drive both near and long-term growth by sharing your customers' success more publicly more often.

Chapter 5
Evolve by Developing a Holistic Trust Model

Core Foundational Elements

Effectively building and maintaining trust requires a holistic approach and involves various strategies beyond customer advocacy.

While several of the core GTM components have been leveraged for a while, given the current research indicating growing vendor skepticism, these tactics now merit review. They should be reviewed relative to your company's current ability to be consistent, authentic and transparent in their use, thereby evaluating if they are most effectively strengthening trust with your stakeholders.

Moreover, it's no longer enough to simply share information once in a sales presentation or have it embedded within your website hoping your audience visits that page on your site. Repeated reminders of your credibility delivered by all your employees through as many channels as possible are recommended to most effectively reach your audience where they today self-educate.

High-Quality Website and Corporate Communications Are you consistent in the way you share your company story? Is how you share your position on DEI or sustainability, for example, consistent in customer communications, employee communications and investor relations? If not, it can cause confusion or mistrust. Or it can be as simple as, are the people on your website limited to senior leadership or AI-generated images? Or do you have your ecosystem's people (employees, customers and partners) showcased?

Even after you achieve attracting your target audience to your site and engage them authentically, it still can be difficult to identify a path to continue to influence them and further build trust to enable growth. I'm keeping an eye on a new tool, RB2B, which provides person-level website visitor identity to identify anonymous website visitors that can push your visitor profiles to Slack in real-time. This is potentially a huge advancement in connecting your company's website activity with identifying follow-on advocacy actions, thereby improving awareness to lead velocity. The RB2B CEO Adam Robinson and Head of Growth Pete Crowley regularly share great insights on LinkedIn for our self-education.

Social Media Engagement
We've talked a lot about social channels already, and with increasing success being garnered through smarter and more robust use of social channels, it's important to ensure optimal leverage.

In addition to customer advocacy, social channels are great for building general brand awareness and recruitment. Employees must be required as part of their job description to proactively build their networks and share industry insights, respond to inquiries, and participate in relevant discussions, which all are components of public trust building. Settling for employees simply 'liking" posts with their network that has aged no longer meets minimum expectations for today's high performing, especially market-facing, team members.

As a reminder, social media presence humanizes a brand and facilitates direct interaction, fostering trust. Many modern CEOs are making great progress with leveraging social media to drive growth, which should be replicated across organizations, leveraging social media to gain reach, increase engagement, generate leads and identify recruits.

Almost every day I read a CEO's post touting their social-selling success. If you're looking for support in building a highly effective CEO LinkedIn program there are several great small consultancies emerging, and #samsales is doing some terrific tactical + practical work on this front and daily share great tips via the LinkedIn profile of their CEO Samantha McKenna.

Awards
Earning awards for your company serves as another proof point and external validation of your team's excellence and commitment to quality.

When stakeholders see that a company has received awards, it reinforces the perception that the company is trustworthy and reliable. This increased credibility can help build trust by reassuring stakeholders that they are dealing with a reputable and competent organization and sets your company apart as a leader in its industry.

Employee morale and engagement is also boosted with awards for employer-related achievements, such as workplace culture, employee benefits, or diversity initiatives. When employees see that their company has been recognized for creating a positive work environment, it reinforces their trust and loyalty to the organization. This, in turn, can lead to higher employee retention rates and increased productivity.

Awards can also have a positive impact on investor confidence. When investors see that a company has been recognized for its products, services, or employer-related practices, it can increase their confidence in the company's ability to deliver value and generate returns. This can lead to greater investor trust and support for the company's growth initiatives.

Industry and Analyst Certifications and Accreditations
Industry-relevant certifications and accreditations demonstrate compliance with standards and best practices. This can be for your product, service or employees. Industry accreditation for individual employees or teams demonstrates the skills and expertise most relevant for success in your industry and a culture that recognizes and enables talent excellence, thereby supporting employee retention and recruitment.

For companies, industry and analyst certifications can reliably confirm alignment with compliance or regulatory requirements which can accelerate deals depending on procurement requirements and processes.

Fairly often I notice announcements of industry and analyst certifications posted by individuals. One tip for companies is to also share your company's multiple points of recognition over time, or even for that year, depending on the type of certifications. For example, in addition to sharing the good news about the one instance of recognition, also include a reference for nine years in a row that you've been recognized with the accreditation. Or for example since 2018, we've been certified. Or Jane Smith is the 15th employee to earn this industry recognition. This confirms consistent excellence and is a far more powerful message than just the one individual posting about their well-deserved recognition.

Partner Relationships
Partnerships allow companies to access expertise, resources, and capabilities beyond your own, which can enhance your ability to deliver value to stakeholders. By collaborating with trusted partners, you demonstrate your commitment to providing comprehensive solutions and meeting stakeholders' needs effectively. Collaborating with partners can foster innovation and facilitate adaptation to market dynamics. By working with external partners who bring different perspectives, technologies, or market insights,

companies stay ahead of the curve and remain competitive.

This commitment to innovation and adaptation can enhance trust by demonstrating your proactive approach to addressing stakeholders' evolving needs and preferences. Partnerships with reputable organizations or industry leaders can also enhance your company's own reputation by association, and by collaborating with nonprofit organizations, government agencies, or community groups, companies can address societal challenges, support local initiatives, and contribute to positive social impact. By promoting and continually sharing this type of partnership engagement, it enhances trust with prospects, customers and employees by showcasing your company's dedication to making a meaningful difference beyond your core business activities.

Customer and Employee Feedback and Satisfaction Surveys
This was touched on earlier but merits a reminder as a basic proven tactic that can easily be implemented. Surveys provide a platform for employees and customers to share their feedback, opinions, and experiences directly with your company. These are effective tools to gain valuable insights into the needs, preferences, and expectations of your employees and customers.

With this understanding you can tailor your products, services, and workplace practices to better meet stakeholder needs, which fosters trust by demonstrating a commitment to customer and employee satisfaction.

Positive survey results on almost any theme - satisfaction, product capabilities, support - are great content to share with prospects and customers. The positive results, which is an aggregation of many voices, can be impactful advocacy. And where possible, always try to share the results back with survey participants in a timely manner, to encourage future survey participation.

Admittedly, again, the above tactics are not new. But, before embarking on a revitalized customer advocacy initiative, it's recommended that you ensure your core components are optimized and that you have the necessary ongoing resource commitment deployed to sustain these efforts. You will build trust through these core elements and will better support the success of your customer advocacy initiative.

Trial, Freemium and Reverse Trial Offers

In addition to a revitalized customer advocacy initiative and the discussed core elements of building trust, there are several advancements around product development, most notably in the SaaS industry, that are emerging as good tools for building public trust and driving growth. These include trial, freemium and reverse trial versions of your product.

These product types are currently most often referenced within industry discussions around emerging product-led revenue (PLG) models, for lowering CAC (customer acquisition cost), better enabling scalability, and providing faster time to value.

But when you dig a bit deeper, they are also addressing the growing skepticism about vendor provided information.

Offering a free trial demonstrates confidence in the quality and effectiveness of your product. By allowing prospects to experience your value firsthand, you build trust by showing that you stand behind your product. A free trial reduces the perceived risk for prospects who may be hesitant to invest in a new solution.

By removing barriers to entry, such as upfront costs or long-term commitments, you make it easier for prospects to try your product, building trust and encouraging adoption. A free trial allows prospects to gain hands- on experience with your product, exploring its features, functionalities, and benefits in a real-world setting. This interactive experience builds trust by enabling prospects to assess the fit and value of your solution for their specific needs.

A free trial also empowers prospects to make informed decisions about whether your product meets their requirements and aligns with their goals.

By providing access to your product's capabilities and performance, you enable prospects to evaluate its suitability and value, fostering trust in your transparency and honesty. Free trials help identify highly qualified leads who have demonstrated interest and intent by opting into the trial. Engagement metrics, such as usage patterns, feature adoption, and feedback, can help prioritize and qualify leads based on their level of interest and likelihood to convert.

A well-executed free trial can also accelerate sales cycles by providing prospects with a direct path to evaluation and purchase. By streamlining the decision-making process and proactively addressing prospects' needs during the trial period, you shorten time-to-value and drive faster conversion, leading to accelerated growth.

There are several SaaS companies who have achieved success by offering free trials to drive growth whose stories are worth checking out, including HubSpot, Zoom, Slack, Trello and Dropbox. Outside of SaaS, we're also seeing good trial success at education companies such as Rosetta Stone (language learning) and LinkedIn Learning (professional development.) By allowing potential customers to experience the value of your products firsthand, companies can attract new users, drive adoption, and ultimately scale businesses effectively.

A freemium version of your product increases accessibility for prospects who may not be ready to commit to a paid solution. By offering a basic, limited-feature version for free, you expand your reach to a broader audience, including those with limited budgets or specific use cases. The freemium version allows prospects to experience the core value proposition of your product without financial commitment. By providing a taste of what your product can do, you build trust by demonstrating its relevance and potential impact on their business.

Freemium models encourage adoption and engagement by lowering barriers to entry and encouraging exploration of additional features or upgrades. As users become familiar with your product and experience its value firsthand, they are more likely to invest in premium offerings or upgrades, driving revenue growth. Freemium models have the potential to facilitate viral growth through word-of-mouth referrals and organic user acquisition.

Satisfied users of the free version may recommend the product to others within their network, expanding your customer base and driving accelerated growth organically. Freemium models also allow you to capture valuable user data and insights about usage patterns, preferences, and behaviors. This data can inform product development, marketing strategies, and sales tactics, enabling you to optimize performance and drive continuous growth.

Several SaaS companies have achieved success by offering freemium versions of their software to drive growth. Some notable examples include Evernote, Bitly, MailChimp, Atlassian (Jira and Confluence), Asana, and SurveyMonkey.

While freemium models are more commonly associated with more traditional technology companies, there have been instances of other types of companies leveraging freemium versions of their software or services to drive growth. A few stories to check out include Duolingo (language learning), Mint (personal finance) and Canva (graphic design.)

Reverse trials, also known as "negative option trials" or "negative option billing," are an online sales tactic used in the software industry where customers are automatically enrolled in a subscription or service at the end of a free trial period unless they actively opt out or cancel the subscription.

Typically, a reverse trial offers a free trial of their product or service for a limited period, such as 7 days or 30 days. During this time, customers can use the software without any cost or obligation. At the end of the free trial period, customers are automatically enrolled in a subscription plan or service agreement unless they take action to cancel or opt out. This means that their credit card will be charged for the subscription fee unless they actively decline the offer.

Customers who do not wish to continue using the software must proactively cancel their subscription before the end of the free trial period to avoid being charged. This typically involves navigating through the software's website or contacting customer support to cancel the subscription.

Reverse trials are somewhat controversial because it includes factoring in the customers' potential inertia or forgetfulness to continue the subscription beyond the free trial period. While they can be an effective way for software companies to acquire new customers and generate recurring revenue, they can also lead to negative customer experiences if customers feel misled or pressured into paying for a service they do not want or need.

It's important for companies to be transparent and ethical in their marketing and sales practices, clearly communicating the terms of any free trials or subscription agreements and making it easy for customers to cancel or opt out if they choose to do so. Some jurisdictions even have regulations governing negative option billing practices, requiring companies to provide clear and conspicuous disclosures, obtain affirmative consent from customers, and offer easy cancellation procedures. Failure to comply with these regulations can result in legal and financial consequences for companies.

Whether you are experimenting with or already leveraging free, freemium or reverse trials, these product strategies can provide value if implemented ethically through authentically building trust and identifying highly qualified leads. Through each, you can provide prospects with hands-on experience, facilitate informed decision-making and enable faster adoption and conversion.

All three options are continuing to offer exciting possibilities for driving growth amidst increasing levels of buyer skepticism.

The Organic Versus Paid Media Debate

For building meaningful trust and engagement, there are differences between organic and paid media that are important to consider. Let's start with another great insight shared on LinkedIn by Sam Jacobs, CEO Pavilion, "We've been testing LinkedIn thought leadership ads. It worked OK so far. We got a few leads. But here's a fun fact… based on the CPM (cost per thousand impressions) ($78), my organic reach on LinkedIn in 2023 was worth about $2,500,000! So, here's my advice for founders and executives… Stop sleeping on LinkedIn. Start posting!"

The net, both organic and paid tactics offer value. In combination, consider it another hybrid approach, you can achieve even greater sustained results, as you are better reaching your audience where they uniquely self-educate.

Today, contrary to strong-held legacy beliefs, paid ads alone will not alone accelerate your growth.

Here's a comparison of the two approaches to help you explore where and how to build your hybrid media plan.

Organic Engagement

Cost
Organic engagement typically requires less financial investment compared to paid strategies. It relies on creating valuable content, optimizing SEO, and building a strong online presence through channels like social media and blogging. As discussed earlier, this is the foundation of revitalizing your customer advocacy efforts.

Credibility
Organic engagement often generates more credibility and trust among B2B audiences. Content that appears organically in search results or is shared by peers is perceived as more authentic and trustworthy.

Long-Term Sustainability
Organic engagement strategies focus on building mutually valued lasting relationships with audiences over time. While it may take longer to see significant results compared to paid tactics, organic engagement

can lead to more sustainable growth and loyalty in the long run.

Content Quality and Relevance
Success with organic engagement depends heavily on creating high-quality, relevant content that addresses the needs and interests of your target audience. This approach requires a deep understanding of your audience's pain points, preferences, and behavior. Leveraging traditional customer advocacy assets, such as case studies, videos and testimonials, can support quality and consistency but should be coupled with authentic commentary from everyone doing the posting.

Paid Engagement

Speed and Reach
Paid engagement strategies offer faster results and broader reach compared to organic methods. By investing in advertising on platforms like Google Ads, LinkedIn Ads, or sponsored content, B2B businesses can quickly increase visibility and reach new audiences.

Targeting and Personalization
Paid engagement allows for precise targeting and personalization based on factors such as demographics, interests, and job titles. This enables B2B businesses to reach highly specific audiences with tailored messaging and offers, with customer advocacy ads aligned by industry, role or use case.

Measurable ROI
Paid engagement provides more immediate and measurable ROI compared to organic strategies. Companies can track metrics such as click-through rates, conversion rates, and cost per acquisition to assess the effectiveness of paid campaigns.

Competition and Cost
Paid engagement can be more competitive and costly, especially in industries with high demand for advertising space. Bidding on popular keywords or targeting competitive audience segments may require a significant budget investment.

When considering your mix of paid versus organic, there are several factors contributing to the decreasing value of paid media and the increasing importance of organic channels in delivering results.

This is yet another nudge for companies to further embrace a more hybrid customer advocacy model to deliver optimal trust-building outcomes in today's business climate.

Ad Saturation
With the proliferation of digital advertising across various platforms, consumers are increasingly bombarded with ads. This oversaturation can lead to ad fatigue, causing users to ignore or actively avoid paid advertisements.

Ad Blockers
The widespread use of ad-blocking software further diminishes the reach and effectiveness of paid media. As more users install ad blockers to avoid intrusive ads, the ability to reach target audiences diminishes.

Declining Trust in Ads
Studies show that consumers are becoming more skeptical of traditional advertising messages and are placing greater trust in organic content. As previously outlined, user-generated reviews, recommendations from current or former colleagues, industry peers and influencer endorsements as trusted proof points prove to be more effective for driving intended buyer behavior.

Changing Algorithms
Social media platforms and search engines frequently update their algorithms to prioritize organic content over paid advertisements. For example, platforms like Facebook and Instagram prioritize posts from friends and family in users' feeds, making it more challenging for paid ads to gain visibility.

Cost Inflation
As competition for ad space increases in parallel with challenging economic factors, the cost of paid media advertising rises accordingly. This can make it difficult for businesses with limited budgets, or financial stress, to achieve a satisfactory return on investment from paid campaigns.

Ad Blindness
Consumers have become adept at tuning out traditional advertisements, whether through banner blindness on websites or skipping commercials on TV and streaming services. This phenomenon makes it increasingly challenging for paid media to capture and hold audience attention.

Content Quality and Relevance
Organic content, such as blog posts, videos, and social media posts, often provides more value to consumers by offering useful information, entertainment, or inspiration. High-quality organic content that resonates with target audiences can drive engagement, shares, and brand loyalty more effectively than paid ads.

Search Engine Optimization (SEO)
As search engines like Google prioritize high-quality, relevant content in search results, businesses that invest in SEO and create valuable organic content can improve their visibility and attract organic traffic without relying solely on paid advertising.

Overall, there is decreasing value of paid media and its associated keyword wars and increasing value on organic tactics. By focusing on building relationships via sharing customer stories in both paid and organic channels, thereby providing value and earning trust, you can better drive sustainable growth and long-term success in today's digital landscape.

Chapter 6
Building Enduring Trust

Over the past 20 years I've marketed more than 200 products for more than 50 different companies generating billions in pipeline to drive revenue growth in both high and low growth markets, most recently with more early-stage companies.

I've personally experienced the GTM revolution, and continue to be intrigued by how new GTM models and capabilities coupled with evolving buyer patterns are impacting stakeholder trust and ultimately growth.

From my research, right now early-stage leaders tend to be more personally present in the market in authentic transparent ways to support building trust. All you must do is look at the Top Voices on LinkedIn. You will find many thought-provoking innovative leaders of small and/or high-growth companies breaking through and very publicly building trust and respect in their industries. Of course, this may be in part due to lack of big marketing budgets.

Nonetheless, they are effectively and efficiently using more modern tactics via the now respected, and increasingly more relied upon, social channels.

Conversely, from my research, the more mature businesses tend to still proportionately rely on traditional methods.

While traditional methods should remain, considering increasing trust erosion, traditional methods can no longer be the entire or primary plan for building and maintaining long-term trust with stakeholders. The data bears this out.

When I first started in B2B marketing, traditional channels were basically all we had for advocacy with digital marketing in its infancy. Trust was established through corporate branding, industry reputation, and face-to-face interactions at trade shows or conferences.

Authentic engagement at that time was limited by the one-way nature of traditional communication channels, with companies controlling the messaging and narrative. Recently, I worked with two CEOs of enterprise software businesses with revenues less than $20M. Their GTM plans were primarily rooted in traditional methods.

Much of our engagement working together was focused around how to employ more modern tactics to break through and address the growing lack of trust from both existing customers and exhibited by their prospects.

The GTM state of these businesses is not unique. By maintaining a dated model that is less authentic, less transparent and less visible, they were actively dismissing the opportunity to build trust with large portions of their audience who have or are moving away from traditional channels. Their prospects had changed their buying patterns to include much more self-education before even speaking to a salesperson and are leaning more into the social channels to self-educate, as these are now perceived as more trusted, as well as more engaging than traditional channels.

Together, we modernized their outdated GTM model that was still based in the assumption that buyers primarily trust and rely upon vendor information to make purchasing decisions.

The rapid acceleration over the last ten years in the digital transformation of GTM models has bypassed many of these more mature companies for a variety of reasons. For early-stage businesses, often it has yet to be deployed. Regardless of the reason, their target markets are now more skeptical of vendors and have evolved in their self-education preferences to rely more on authentic, peer-based platforms. This is evidenced through the latest research, and amidst the growing lack of trust in vendor supplied information.

As discussed in detail throughout this book, primarily through the lens of customer advocacy, trust-building proof points must repeatedly be shared with your audience. This can, in large part, be achieved with a company-wide revitalization of your customer advocacy initiative.

In larger or more mature businesses, while a senior leader or two may believe this is important, the biggest challenge I continue to see is in its execution. You may have the team, tools and budget. But you don't have the plan, training or internal energy yet for rallying your many team members to make the necessary change and embrace their role in the daily implementation of customer advocacy aligned to your growth strategies.

For early-stage businesses, you may not yet have the team, tools and a big budget, but you understand the importance of modern trust-building communications. You want to get started with building a foundation with your existing resources, including having direct CEO involvement, but you're not sure where to get started. In both scenarios, this is where my advisory services support businesses.

In working with your organization, we borrow from the great Simon Sinek by starting with inspiring your teams with your why. And then we integrate into your training how and what each team member needs to do to effectively contribute to building trust for your company, centered on the near and long-term impact that can be achieved via a company-wide hybrid customer advocacy initiative.

With the growing lack of trust continuing to provide increasing headwinds for B2B growth, I encourage you to reach out to and research the many resources that have been provided to evaluate for yourself what is best for your business. The resources are included to support your self-education and hopefully provide a few nuggets of insight to guide you in your journey to strengthening trust for your business.

My ultimate lesson so far in my journey is that whatever GTM strategy is employed, organizations must commit to the ongoing company-wide strengthening of - public - trust, including incorporating trust-building responsibilities in all employee job descriptions.

Regardless of the evolving business landscape, including the use of AI and other emerging innovations and trends, companies that prioritize public trust-building efforts will have enduring authentic relationships, continually deliver value, and drive accelerated growth in today's AI world.

Reference Sites

Thank you to all the big thinkers and their organizations who inspire me, and I learn from every day.

Atlassian
atlassian.com

Adweek
adweek.com

Asana
asana.com

Basecamp
basecamp.com

Bizzabo
bizzabo.com

Bitly
bitly.com

Boston Consulting Group
bcg.com

Buffer
buffer.com

Bureau of Labor Statistics
bls.gov

Canva
canva.com

ChatGPT
chatgtp.com

Chief Executive
chiefexecutive.net

Constellation Research
constellationr.com

Digital Third Coast
digitalthirdcoast.com

Dropbox
dropbox.com

Duolingo
duolingo.com

Edelman
edelman.com

Employee Benefits Research Institute
ebri.org

Evernote
evernote.com

Facebook
facebook.com

Forbes
forbes.com

Forrester
forrester.com

G2
G2.com

Gallup
gallup.com

Google
google.com

Great Place to Work
greatplacetowork.com

Harvard Business Review
hbr.com

Hootsuite
hootsuite.com

HubSpot
hubspot.com

LinkedIn
linkedin.com

MailChimp
mailchimp.com

Marketing Week
marketingweek.com

Mint
mint.com

OptinMonster
optinmonster.com

Oracle
oracle.com

Pavillion
joinpavillion.com

PWC
pwc.com

Pierre Herubel
pierreherubel.com

RB2B
rb2b.com

Rosetta Stone
rosettastone.com

Salesforce
salesforce.com

Sam Sales Consulting
samsalesconsulting.com

Slack
slack.com

SurveyMonkey
surveymonkey.com

The Think Tank
thinktank.org.uk

Trello
trello.com

Workday
workday.com

Zendesk
zendesk.com

Zoom
zoom.com

Copyright © 2024 Kristin Oelke

Made in the USA
Middletown, DE
29 June 2024